FEMININE POWER™

Fully access your supreme birthright.

Welcome and reclaim this intrinsic privilege while living in harmonious balance between the masculine and the feminine.

FEMININE POWER COPYRIGHT

Copyright © 2010-2013 by Miranda J. Barrett.
Original Concept Copyright © 2008 by Miranda J. Barrett.
Copyright © 2010 Front Cover Artwork by Helena Nelson-Reed.

All rights reserved. This book may not be reproduced in whole or in part without written permission. In accordance with the U.S. Copyright act of 1976, the scanning, uploading and electronic sharing of any part of this book without permission of the publisher is unlawful piracy and theft of the author's intellectual property.

If you would like to use material from the book (other than for review purposes), prior written permission must be obtained by contacting either the publisher at:

Info@ MirandaJBarrett.com
or the artist at www.HelenaNelsonReed.com
Thank you for the support of the author and the artist's rights.

Please note:

The written or spoken information, ideas, procedures and suggestions contained and presented in 'FEMININE POWER' workshops and books are meant for educational purposes only and are not for diagnosis. It should not be used as a substitute for your physician's advice. 'FEMININE POWER' is not therapy and is not intended to replace the recommendations of a licensed health practitioner. It is the responsibility of the reader to consult with their own medical Doctor, Counselor, Therapist or other competent professional regarding any condition before adopting any of the suggestions in this book.

FEMININE POWER™

Dedicated to the silent stirrings of Feminine Power, which resides within the womb, heart and magnificent Glory known as Woman.

MISSION STATEMENT

To guide and facilitate women
in becoming their most beautiful and radiant selves.

To acknowledge and embrace the well of love
and power which lies within all women and to ignite the
awakening and embodying of this life force.

To empower each woman, through exquisite self-care and love,
to live her fullest life possible, and to walk her path of wisdom
and truth, as she shares this light and knowledge
with all beings.

IN DEEP GRATITUDE
Thank you

The creation, birth and life of 'A Woman's Truth' would not have been possible without the love, support and devotion from the following angels in my life:

My beautiful daughter Megan who naturally embodies the teachings of living in her truth and integrity, thank you for the creative gift of the beautiful artwork. Helena Nelson-Reed for her generosity of spirit in allowing her extraordinary artwork, which embodies the teachings so magnificently, to grace the covers. Dennise Marie Keller for her unwavering support and dedication to the teachings and for proofing, editing, aligning and translating my vision into the technical world of manifestation. Dan Fowler for his creative genius and dedication. Lucy Alexander and Suzanne Ryan, my dearest friends for their amazing editing and wholehearted encouragement. Monica Marsh for her commitment, support and belief in the workshops. Maggie Crawford, my mum, for her proofing and for being a living example of the teachings. Cait Myer and Katie Steen for their patience and ability to decipher my handwriting and for formatting the books. Bethany Kelly for her support. Deborah Waring for holding the space for the conception of 'A Woman's Truth' to be born and for her insight in the first year of teaching and Emmanuel for believing in my vision.

My mentors and teachers Rod Stryker, Adyashanti and Alison Armstrong, Max Simon and Jeffrey Van Dyk for their continuous and guiding light in my life, their never-ending belief in my potential and for always teaching me the way to evolve into my highest and most potent self. And to all of you beautiful and courageous women who are committing to living your truth and transforming into your most radiant selves,

thank you.

A PRELUDE

An overture to embodying feminine power.

It feels a deep honor to be Miranda's witness for Feminine Power. I have known Miranda since we were children and have seen her transform and become the wise woman she now is. As she so honestly describes, by telling you parts of her own story, it is only by facing and feeling our wounds from our past and uncovering our ancestral pain can we discover and embody who we truly are.

There is no quick way, and Miranda gives a clear step by step approach to the dialogue with the different aspects of ourselves. Only then, by casting off their critical, wounded voices can you start accessing your intuitive wisdom.

~ Miranda Carey
Equine facilitated Psychotherapy
Psychotherapeutic Counselor and Supervisor.

In this book, Miranda really explains the practical aspects of respecting our feminine powers. She really has amazing exercises and insights into living a balanced life. Miranda spells out the under discussed notion of self-care, a topic which makes many women scratch their heads and say, ' Self-care? For me?'

She answers with a resounding yes! Bravo for a much needed manual on our sacred feminine energy and practical ways to unleash her!

~ Lorraine Roe
Psychic, Author, Huffington Post Blogger
www.psychichousewives.com

FEMININE POWER™

Gems of Love

FEMININE POWER	1
YIN YANG	6
AN ODE TO THE FEMININE	10
A DREAM OR A REALITY?	15
ASPECTS AND PERSONAS	16
LEARNING TO LISTEN	19
CREATE AN INTUITIVE COUNCIL	21
THE MOTHER OF US ALL	32
HOW TO DIGNIFY THE FEMININE	36
HONORING YOUR FEMININE	46
HOW TO EXALT THE MASCULINE	48
HONORING YOUR MASCULINE	54
HOW TO CELEBRATE THE CHILD	56
HONORING YOUR CHILD	64
HOW TO REVERE THE HIGHER SELF	66
HONORING YOUR HIGHER SELF	69

FULL EXPRESSION OF YOUR FEMININE 71
REVEAL MORE TRUTH 74

A DAILY PRACTICE
Commit to Yourself

*F*ollow these simple steps daily as a way to instill and strengthen your heartfelt resolve to love yourself. This will help to keep you aligned, transforming and on track, giving you a stable foundation for the rest of your life. As a gift to yourself, please mark the teachings as you read them through and congratulate yourself with each one. See each day as a commitment to take exquisite care of yourself.

- ◊ DAY ONE: FEMININE POWER 1
- ◊ DAY TWO: YIN YANG 6
- ◊ DAY THREE: AN ODE TO THE FEMININE 10
- ◊ DAY FOUR: A DREAM OR A REALITY? 15
- ◊ DAY FIVE: ASPECTS AND PERSONAS 16
- ◊ DAY SIX: LEARNING TO LISTEN 19
- ◊ DAY SEVEN: CREATE AN INTUITIVE COUNCIL 21
- ◊ DAY EIGHT: THE MOTHER OF US ALL 32
- ◊ DAY NINE: HOW TO DIGNIFY THE FEMININE 36
- ◊ DAY TEN: HONORING YOUR FEMININE 46
- ◊ DAY ELEVEN: HOW TO EXALT THE MASCULINE 48
- ◊ DAY TWELVE: HONORING YOUR MASCULINE 54
- ◊ DAY THIRTEEN: HOW TO CELEBRATE THE CHILD 56
- ◊ DAY FOURTEEN: HONORING YOUR CHILD 64

- ◊ DAY FIFTEEN: HOW TO REVERE THE HIGHER SELF 66
- ◊ DAY SIXTEEN: HONORING YOUR HIGHER SELF 69
- ◊ DAY SEVENTEEN: FULL EXPRESSION OF YOUR FEMININE 71
- ◊ DAY EIGHTEEN: REVEAL MORE TRUTH 74

A Life Worth Living

*"Never give from your well.
Always give from your overflow."*
~ Rumi

All too often as women, your own needs are denied for the benefit of others as you orchestrate your life through demands and expectations you feel responsible for. Unfortunately, this can leave you without the juice and energy needed to be present fully and to enjoy life. During these readings, you will continually discover more about who you truly are and learn the tools needed to live your most authentic and fulfilling life possible. From this place, you will experience being 'full to overflowing' and all the joy and energy this brings.

As you delve into these teachings, you will explore, laugh, study, share, and freely express who you are. In this sacred space, you will ultimately learn your truth as a woman in order to shine, to embody your own beauty, believe in your own worth, and take exquisite care of yourself. For only in this way can you truly be of service.

During these guidebooks, many of the basic needs of women will be explored such as sleep, nutrition, creativity, movement and time to replenish. A topic has been chosen for each book and a cohesive and practical foundation is laid out to inspire and guide you. This will bring about a new strength and resolve which will allow your needs to become a priority, without letting your outer world dictate otherwise. By the end of our time together, the concept of being confident, loving, serene and passionate will no longer be a distant fantasy. Instead, these and many other extraordinary qualities that you naturally embody as a woman will flow with ease, grace and love.

With life's demands so high, it has become imperative that your needs are first acknowledged, honored and then taken care of. From this vantage point, your relationship with yourself then has the potential to be transformed into one of self-love. The beauty is this in turn creates a life that not only fulfills you and your life's purpose, but also allows everyone touched by your presence to receive this gift.

I look forward to spending this precious time with you.

Welcome to A Woman's Truth.

Sincerely and with love,

FEMININE POWER
For the love of women.

Feminine Power is born through the recognition and honoring of the vital essence of the Feminine. This majestic birthright will manifest in your life when you give this powerful and fundamental nature of your being high value and a worthy place in your daily existence. When you live in accordance with this legacy of Feminine strength and ability, you are living in balance as nature intended.

The essential heart force of the Feminine is all about being, yet unfortunately, western society is raised and heavily orientated around the Masculine energy, which is all about doing. Therefore, life tends to embody qualities that are more masculine. This leaves the essence of Feminine energy often devalued and accepted as limiting or insignificant. These negating patterns become ingrained in the conscious and unconscious mind, therefore making it difficult to even recognize their existence and even harder to rise above them.

For women, these restrictive beliefs create a division between a natural way of being and the way you are taught to behave. This separation destroys self-worth and results in the denial of your True Self. Instead, you become a mistress of adaptation and work hard to become what you think you *should* be in order to be accepted.

Self-worth has a huge impact in determining your life. Its opinion results in either the approval or disapproval of the self. The repercussion is the degree to which you believe yourself to be capable, worthy and significant. Most importantly, your self-worth defines how you relate to yourself and the people in your life. If you or another regards you as inconsequential and not important, your self-worth as a woman will also diminish. These societal conditionings and expectations placed upon your role as a woman will bury the limitless power that lies deep inside of you.

For a woman to raise her worth, it is vital first to recognize the behavior patterns imposed on you by both yourself and society. Unfortunately, many of these opinions are highly destructive to the Feminine essence. These beliefs have the impact of making you feel as though you are weak and powerless. By becoming acutely aware of what detrimental judgments you may be holding, you can then choose to release them and connect to the Truth of who you really are.

what does it mean to be a woman in today's world?

Many women have a distorted view of who they are and how they should behave. Your ancestors, society, tradition or culture and even your immediate family can certainly play a role in defining what or how your Feminine or Masculine side is playing out. For women, there is no longer the comfort or security of knowing exactly what part to play or how to play it. While your grandmothers were willing to live by the limitations, as tradition once clearly dictated, today the choice of how to express your femininity can be endlessly creative. In fact, the role of being female in today's world is often one of reinvention.

As you remember how to reclaim your power and creative expression, you then get to choose. For some women you may want to stretch beyond the realms of your home and family. For others the choice is to embody your power by being a mother or partner. The gift of living in this culture at this time is that you can even choose to be both. Whatever the decision, know that you have the power and ability to recreate the collective role of women. It is truly a dynamic and pioneering time!

While this all sounds good on paper, in reality, until the baggage from the past is cleared, none of this is easily realized. Your life experiences, which may have resulted in wounds, anger or rejection can easily become internalized and can relinquish your power as a woman.

Yet, if you have the courage to look inside of yourself and to question some of the old and unhealthy beliefs, your observations can blossom into awareness and further reveal and clarify the internal work needing to be done.

Living in Shadows Past.

How often have you loathed yourself and given your power away?

How often have you sworn never to do the same again?

What is this pattern ingrained within you of blaming yourself or others

and giving away your essence to memories of what was?

Can you see the opportunity to choose differently?

Are you ready to free yourself from the bondage of the past?

Are you ready to live in the present moment

without feeling obligated to some old patterns and beliefs?

Are you ready to express your essence honestly?

Will you choose to be in the moment when darkness clouds all reason?

Shadows of the past cannot exist less you embrace them.

Are you ready to live your life in the now and invite in a new and hope filled future?

Remember, you always have a choice to love and honor yourself.

The beauty is that as you clarify and clear these old impressions upon your life,

you become more in control of who you are and how you choose to be.

In essence, your True Self begins to shine.

So what actually is the Feminine
and more importantly, what does it mean to be a woman
embodying her Feminine power in today's world?

The following pages will answer these questions and lead you on a journey of discovery to your own precious relationship with the Feminine.

Curiously, when a woman is living in her power, she will not only witness Feminine aspects of being, but also Masculine qualities as well. Women already embody both the Masculine and Feminine. The same is true of men and all things on this earth plane.

There is a theory that human existence relies on the balance of polarities. If you recall the yin and yang symbol, you will see a fluid melding of these influences within the whole. Each aspect has its place and center. There is much to ponder about this symbol.

To inquire which parts of your personality embody one or both of these qualities will certainly give you insight and a way to journey back to a place of balance and harmony in yourself. This practice will allow you to access your full power and potential in a Feminine body.

Practically speaking, with so much confusion and change surrounding the roles of men and women in today's society, trying to be Feminine can seem a far-off cry. Especially after a full day of multitasking, work and a 'to do' list as long as your arm you may feel that is impossible In fact, women often let their external life dictate and carry on regardless, instead of pausing and resting even after exhaustion has set in. Masculine energy is what you use to get the job done! This can deplete you even more. Obviously, there are times when it is appropriate to be in the role of doing yet, in this culture, the Masculine side of the coin can certainly be overrated and overused. If not balanced by the Feminine, it can take over as the only way to accomplish and get things done.

Actually, the same choice or action can be carried out by following either a Feminine or a Masculine impulse. There is a Feminine way of doing a chore and a Masculine way to accomplish the same result. The simple act of putting on some of your favorite music while doing the dishes can invoke a more Feminine atmosphere and transform a chore into a more enjoyable experience.

How you choose to carry out an action, whether it be with the more Feminine or Masculine approach, will influence the quality of the energy required to complete the experience. The quest is to honor and invoke the Feminine and the Masculine when or wherever you deem appropriate. There is no right or wrong here. It is always about which choice will empower and enliven you.

*If something increases your life force, then do more of it
and if something decreases your life force, then do less of it.*

On some occasions, you will be acutely aware and understand the choices you make and where they stem from. Other times you will unconsciously just be in either the Feminine or Masculine, because it naturally feels right or gives you pleasure. Then there will always be moments where a different choice could have been more appropriate. A wise person is one who lives and learns by their mistakes.

At the germ of creation, the Feminine and the Masculine are balanced in each one of us, regardless of our gender. In life, as we move towards our birthright and true calling, a balance of both the Feminine and the Masculine energies will yield harmony, fulfillment, happiness, prosperity and true abundance.

☯ YIN YANG ☯

A balance between the Masculine and the Feminine, the light and the shadow.

Yin and Yang are opposing energies comprised of the whole. Everything in this world is interconnected and has both the Yin and the Yang aspects. At times one element may manifest more strongly than the other may. Yet there is always a constant flow between the two and it can never exist in absolute stasis.

Yin and Yang symbolize balance in all things; light and dark, male and female, positive and negative, good and bad and is a constant reminder that all aspects of yourself need to be honored to maintain the delicate balance in your life.

It is often human nature to deny one or both of these aspects. Unfortunately, this can create a push or pull of energies resulting in conflict, leaving you feeling drained or stressed in order to maintain control over the aspect you are favoring. There can even be conflicts in nature as one element pushes and the other pulls: The sun rises as the moon sets, the tides ebb and flow, you are born and you die. The cycle of energy is constant, ever evolving and must be honored in order to maintain a sense of equilibrium.

The moon, the earth, water, femininity and nighttime often symbolize the Yin quality. It is also represented as soft, yielding, slow, cold, tranquil, peaceful, and scattered and the void. In comparison, Yang symbolizes the sun, the sky, fire, masculinity and daytime. It represents fast, hard, solid, focus and aggression.

Yin and Yang are opposing yet dependent forces that flow in a natural cycle, always seeking balance. Though contrasting, they are not in competition with one another. They are merely two aspects of the whole. As women, it is vital to honor your Masculine as much as your Feminine, in order to be true to yourself. This balance brings with it peace, joy and happiness by honoring all of who you are.

One cannot be, without the other.

BECOMING THE OPPOSITE

when opposites attract balance becomes easy to resist.

It seems to be a part of human nature to hide or limit certain aspect of our true nature, often as a way to survive. Yet when it becomes appropriate to release this banished part of you out of the shadows finally, she can often reveal herself rather like a banshee, starved of the light, craving the attention and becoming an amplified version of the prisoner.

Therefore, by the law of physics, when something is held in an extreme and is finally released, there is often a natural, yet severe pendulum swing in the opposite direction. The momentum back and forth will seem intense, until eventually, you rest back into the center of whom you truly are. Your emotions are no different.

Identify Where You Are Living In Your Opposite:

◈ Are you aware of having an aspect of yourself that has been in exile?

◈ Have you ever embraced a part of yourself that has been shut down?

◆ What did you notice when you invited this part back into your whole being?

◆ What aspect of yourself have you been ignoring and punishing? This could be your creative, playful or even your disciplined side.

◆ Is there more than one aspect that you have been avoiding?

◆ Are you ready to reveal these hidden parts of yourself?

Remember this takes courage because there was a reason you stuffed her in the basement in the first place. She was too wild, too demanding, too big, too afraid, too something! Courage comes from the heart. Therefore, it will be out of a love or respect for yourself that you are willing and able to acknowledge and honor all of who you are. When you reveal these aspects, it is vital to meet them with love and compassion. Let these two salves be the sweet gentle wisdom to encourage these hidden aspects back into the light.

Know there will be a reaction and it may not be pretty. As already mentioned a swing to the opposite extreme may occur. Therefore, if you have been imprisoning your wild opinionated bitch, when you finally unshackle her, she may well have quite a lot to say and express!

Imagine you were drowning and as you were pulled from the water and your stomach pumped, you would throw up and gasp for air because your life depended on it. When releasing a drowned, gagged and bound part of your being, the response will be no different.

"In my youth I lived deeply and darkly in my inner bitch and wild side, not caring much what others thought. Yet strangely, throughout this time I also took beautiful and loving care of a dying father, which revealed to me this world of polar opposites. While living in England, I would often walk past construction sites. The normal reaction from the builders was to wolf whistle and make comments to young, pretty girls. Instead, I always received a comment along the lines of 'try smiling love'! This simple statement revealed much of my state of mind it seemed.

Then when I became pregnant with my daughter, I decided in order to become a good mother I needed to capture and imprison this untamed part of my being. In her place I devotedly invoked love, discipline, hard work, patience, security and as much safety as I could muster. I dedicated myself to this practice for many years. Yet occasionally I would feel the stirrings of my wild side. I channeled her into spiritual practices and hard work.

I then reached a place in my life where the yearning for balance needed to be honored. Over the last few years, I have been inviting in and revealing the inner wisdom of my wilder nature. The gift is with life experience, I now know she will not try to sabotage and destroy all I have built. Yet it is vital that I let her run free and express on what seems to be a very regular basis." ~ Miranda

AN ODE TO THE FEMININE

'Ah, The Feminine …' mused the Masculine.

A look of awe and slight bewilderment across his face.

'The Feminine…

The bearer and holder of such beauty, strength, and power,

Such intuitive wisdom and mystery,

Such sensuality and light,

Yet, such vulnerability and tenderness.

To love her

To lay in her arms

To hold her

To know she is happy.

Yet, is this a dream?

Or will I wake to a world of hard, cold will

With steel walls to climb and battles to win?

In this world

If I am tired,

She will nourish me.

If I am wounded,

She will heal me.

To be in the presence of the Source of us all,
To be before the Goddess, the Seer,
The sheer embodiment of beauty itself.

I bask in her Presence.
I become stronger and more powerful
With her at my side.
With her in her power,
Fully embodied, nourished and whole,
Shining like the moon of the winter solstice,
I remember myself.
I know my Purpose.
I see myself in her.

Yet, when she tires from nourishing and giving to others over herself,
I no longer feel her light.
When she depletes her life force by giving it all away,
Instead of receiving our bounty and love for her
She fades.
I no longer see
Her power,
Her strength,
Her light.
It is as though she has doused herself.

The flame fades.

And instead of love meeting my heart,

I feel anger and resentment.

Oh, where has she gone?

My Feminine.

My love.

My beauty.

Lost to the underworld.

And in my heartbreak

I see her unhappiness,

Her misery,

Her disconnection from me and ultimately her Self.

And I ask,

In fact, I implore,

Are you brave enough to take care of yourself?

Are you strong enough to say no?

Are you powerful enough to ask for what you need?

So you can shine again

And be all of who you truly are.

I know you are strong enough.

I see your power.

I know who you are.

And I pray for your return,

My Love, my Queen.

I pray for you to love and exquisitely nourish yourself

With the same grace and generosity that you give to us all.

I pray for you to remember your Truth,

Your bountiful heart,

Your needs,

Your utter beauty.

I pray for you to take such exquisite and beautiful care of yourself

That you are always open to receiving all the love and adoration that is

Present for you.

Allow me to share with you.

Allow me to support you in your passions.

Allow me to hold space for you in your darkest moments.

Allow me to fill your life with light as you have filled mine.

Allow me…

To pray with you…

Allow me.

I ask this of you, dear one.

For our sake,

And the happiness and well-being of all those who swim

In the lake of your exquisite energies.

So that we may receive the nectar of your presence,

The love of your soul,

And the beauty of who you truly are.

Ah, The Feminine…' mused the Masculine.

'To be loved by her.'

A DREAM OR A REALITY?
Being in your Feminine power.

When women accept that dreaming and creativity are as important as career and goals, they become good listeners and begin speaking more eloquently. That being of service is a quality resulting in so much more than the meaningless pursuit of material gain. That ageless wisdom resulting from experience and living, is more valuable than the knowledge acquired from books and universities. Only then will you be living in your Feminine power.

When the day comes that women no longer feel the need to compete with one another, instead finding grace and beauty in each other's presence, then you will have discovered your Feminine power. When giving a compliment born from the heart and a smile of support to any woman who crosses your path, then you will have sourced your Feminine power. The natural result of taking exquisite care of yourself allows you to be full to overflowing, and then you will have birthed your Feminine power. When you acknowledge with love, your need for support, teamwork and collaboration in order to blossom, then you will be in this infinite source.

When you acknowledge your nurturing abilities and cease viewing them as a hindrance for your advancement and growth, then you will be an embodiment of this life force. Once you start living this way, you will become truly powerful and a symbol of the natural beauty and magnificence of being a women.

As you begin to rebirth your infinite, internal power and gain true, high self-worth, you will finally be living without the constant conflict between your inner and outer worlds. This will be the way of the world when women fully live in their power.

"The world will be saved by the Western woman."
~ Dalai Lama

ASPECTS AND PERSONAS
who am I really?

Each and every one of us possesses aspects that need to be honored, heard and acknowledged. Some of these personas will serve you well, yet others can lead you down a path of destruction. The point is to pause long enough to inquire into why the demand is happening, which can give you deep insight into what may be out of balance in your life. The trouble begins when an unconscious or wounded aspect from the past starts to run the show. Often this will result in behaviors that can seem childish or overly emotional. Even though some part of you may be watching and wondering why you are behaving this way, it is seems as though the train of strange and erratic behavior has already left the station.

"When I am overworked and not giving myself enough down time, my childish aspect will rise from the depths and become extremely rebellious and opinionated. She loves to swear and do the opposite of whatever she should be doing. On the one hand, if I give her too much power, her swearing, sugar and playing would take over my world. Yet if the adult in me actually pauses from work long enough to see what the child really needs, it will often be revealed that I have not had a full day off for quite a while. This results in my life becoming riddled with responsibility and stress.

In reality, at this point, the upset child is my teacher. "Enough" she is imploring. "Stop. All work and no play makes Miranda a very dull girl!" At this point, if I am wise, I will organize some down time to be. No timeline, no agenda, and no shackles of responsibilities are on my plate. It is similar to letting the wild pony run for a while. The good news is, with age and hopefully some wisdom, this aspect can be released of all containment and restriction of being a "grown up", but you can still keep yourself safe. Usually if I make time to let her play, the swearing, attitude and sugar frenzy relax and her innocent, joyful qualities begin to shine. And it seems as though the people in my life thoroughly enjoy her!" ~ Miranda

The vital component is to acknowledge what is driving the unconscious behavior causing this discontent. In this case, of working too hard, it is a fear of survival that there will not be enough money or resources to support loved ones.

What is being offered here is to become conscious and to no longer ignore certain aspects or personas that you embody. As a human being, you are a miraculous spectrum of the whole. You have the ability to love, create and to truly be of service, yet you can swing into hate, destruction and greed in a heartbeat. Often when the harsher qualities rear their heads, it seems as though fear or survival are running the show.

Therefore, the vital component is having the courage to look fear or unhappiness directly in the eye, because this masterful teacher should not be ignored.

Ask Yourself The Following Questions:

◆ *Of what am I afraid?*

◆ *How is my survival being threatened?*

◆ *What is the worst-case scenario? What is your deepest fear?*

◆ Why am I so afraid of this possibility?

◆ What do I know to be true in this situation?

◆ What is a possible solution?

Miracles can happen when you choose to pause for a moment to ask these questions and then be still long enough to listen to the answers.

Often your true self or higher mind has a brilliant solution. Just as an adult would calm the fearful and irrational child by turning on the light in the bedroom, this simple act would show her that the wild serpent in the shadows was actually her dressing gown cord. Likewise, the adult aspect of the Self can reassure your own survival personality when she feels all alone and is allowing the fantasy and vision in her head to explode into a world of terrors, whether it is a fear of snakes, money, abandonment or death.

LEARNING TO LISTEN
can you hear me?

With the pace of life moving quickly from one moment to the next, all too often it is difficult to truly take the time to listen.

The female brain is designed with an acute ability to multitask. She therefore tends to hear process and interpret information at an extremely rapid pace. Although this is a crucial survival skill, unfortunately it can lead to vital pieces of a conversation being missed. And as you may have noticed, this can result in misunderstandings and possible arguments.

Often, the essential piece, which is not heard, can lead to a button being pushed in the other person, particularly if it was an important part of the communication. This can cause frustration and an even greater break down in the ability to connect with each other, leading to hurt feelings, anger and drama. How often have you uttered the words, 'you are not listening to me' or had someone say this to you?

It seems the valuable gift of this ancient form of communication has become lost in today's fast pace and modern world of technology. Regrettably, the act of *listening* has become a forgotten art form or was possibly never learned.

"I have a dear and wise friend, who posted on her dating profile she was interested in a man who did not deem texting as a basis of a relationship!" ~ Miranda

Real listening requires you to be present with whom you are having a conversation:

◆ Listening means you need to slow down.

◆ Take the time to open your heart.

◆ Make eye contact.

◆ Allow your senses to be focused on the other person.

◆ Perceive what the other is saying is important, even if you disagree!

◆ Do not interrupt.

◆ Pay attention to how you may be mentally formulating your response to another's story, even before they have finished speaking. A sure sign of not listening to the other!

◆ Wait for the other person to finish, which could mean a moment of silence.

Letting go of the awkwardness of silence and learning to be comfortable in its presence is a vital component to listening. In these precious moments, you will find that your relationship with the person in front of you will shift from one of separation into one of partnership, which is always a beautiful gift. When you are calm and in the moment, it will allow others to slow down and be present. By choosing to ignore your inner chatter about what you have to do, or worrying about the past or future, you will be able to listen actively in the present. Remember, listening takes practice. It will involve precious moments of silence, which is good as you pause long enough to see if they have finished talking.

Most importantly, you need to have some juice and energy of your own to be present fully, ready and able to listen completely to another. If you are over flooded with your own emotions, stories and grievances, there will not be enough space to be present and listen to another's.

CREATE AN INTUITIVE COUNCIL

*By aligning, balancing and communicating
with each aspect of your Self, all things are possible.*

This Council is a powerful and life changing technique. The intention is to introduce you lovingly to the individual aspects of the Self, the Feminine, the Masculine and the Child. Once experienced, this safe and revealing space will allow you to maintain a personal and balanced relationship between these precious facets of human existence. It seems when any of these personas are being ignored, disrespected, dishonored or undervalued, you can lose sight of your higher purpose and calling, as well as the ability to achieve it.

As a human being, you are made up of many different parts and when one is overlooked, ultimately an imbalance occurs. This Council offers you the gift of acknowledging and embodying all aspects of yourself, the good, the bad and the ugly, therefore, allowing the full spectrum of your being to be present and fully active in your life.

Be patient with yourself during this process, especially if this kind of work is new to you. Just like learning a new language or getting to know someone, it can be clumsy or awkward at times or bring up feelings and experiences from your past. Know this and trust that this is part of your healing and your journey to return to the True Self and it is truly an honorable one.

The following method can be invited into all areas of your life. You might use the Council while you are walking, journaling, talking with a friend or having a full-on conversation with yourself. For those of you with a meditation practice, it can always be incorporated into your routine. The most potent time is when you are in a state of conflict or confusion. It will bring clarity to the situation and a productive way forward.

In the beginning, bestow yourself with the gift of using these techniques on a regular basis, until you become familiar and friends with all of yourself. It is also wise to breathe into the process and choose a time when you are not feeling rushed. With practice, this dialogue will become natural and an effortless part of whom you are.

The definition of a 'Council' is a body of persons specially designed or selected to act in an advisory capacity. In other words, they are there to consult and advise.

The good news is you have all of this and more already inside of you. Imagine that!

*"If the freedom of speech is taken away
then dumb and silent we may be led, like sheep to the slaughter."*
~ George Washington

"When I first started to explore my own personal relationship between these two possible polarities of the Feminine and the Masculine, I was shocked and honestly dismayed that my Feminine and Masculine were actually at war with each other. In fact, they reminded me of divorcing parents; hurt, angry, resentful, not being heard and certainly not getting their individual needs met. In fact, they both seemed exhausted, irritable and at the end of their tether. How I accomplished anything was a miracle to me because it seemed as though they were incapable of working together in partnership. Have you ever had that feeling of being pulled in two directions, one with a banshee wail, the other with a pounding fist and a shout? With this dynamic in tow, to move forward with any insight, clarity or peace seems close to impossible.

After spending some time getting to know these two opposing aspects of myself, I realized that both sides actually had the same concern in common. The Feminine and the Masculine were desperately trying to keep me safe, help me survive and express their individual needs to allow and make this happen. Unfortunately, their role models were often from the family line that had displayed a distorted view of how to achieve the outcome of a healthy relationship. The result was pretty much a stalemate with some highflying emotions and resentments thrown in.

With patience, awareness and by setting the intention to come from a place of deep gratitude for all they had tried to accomplish over the years, a long slow journey back to partnership began. By listening and respecting their differences, they began seeing how their values were actually similar. This allowed them to set their common goal as one and embrace all of these extraordinary and powerful aspects that both the Feminine and the Masculine have to offer." ~ Miranda

"We must keep both our femininity and our strength."
~ Indra Devi

SETTING UP THE COUNCIL
A Sacred Space.

During this Council it is vital to establish a safe and hallowed space in your mind. It is a sacred circle, which represents all aspects of you, comments or ideas. Nothing is excluded or deemed inappropriate, as long as it fits within the Council structure and guidelines. This conscious freedom allows each speaker to reveal his or her deepest thoughts or feelings free from censorship or judgment. The word *sacred* cannot be stressed enough.

Be clear to set the intention for the Council to be a revered and an honorable one before you begin the process.

The Guidelines Are Simple And Keep The Space Safe:

◆ Everyone is allowed time to express their thoughts and feelings.

◆ No one has to speak.

◆ One voice is heard at a time and no one is allowed to interrupt another.

◆ Each holds a sacred space for the other.

◆ Remain in the present and in a receptive, listening stance.

To Begin The Council:

◆ **Take a moment to imagine yourself as being the observer of the Council you are setting up. This witness aspect of you is the part that is intending the Council and setting the stage.**
This will give the arena a safe referee and advocate for the guidelines and you may respectfully step in at any time if the parameters are not being followed. See yourself as the mediator or guide.

◆ **Invite the Feminine, the Masculine and the Self into the Council arena.**
Your Child aspect may also want to participate.

◆ **Ask all parties to agree on the Council format, including abiding by all the guidelines and intentions.**
If any aspect has an issue, allow these to be voiced and heard. As the overseer, inquire to find out what this facet needs to feel safe and comfortable enough to continue.

◆ **If you are a visual person, you may get a clear image of the Council setting.**
It could be inside or outside, a luxurious hotel room, a meadow or even a courthouse. Do not judge what comes up. This is all about allowing your subconscious mind to reveal itself.

◆ **Begin the discussion with a moment of silence and see who is to begin.**
Again, if more than one person has something to express at the same time, as the mediator ask if they are willing to take turns and find out who is comfortable to go second. Everyone will all have a turn and a say.

◆ **You might open the arena by asking, 'What is it that you have to say?'**
Remember this is about everyone listening. Now is not the time to argue or give an opinion. If any of the Council does not care for what is being said, encourage them to continue listening and remind them they will have their time to voice an opinion.

◆ **When an aspect is speaking, they may have plenty to say or they may need encouragement. If so, you as the mediator can ask some questions.**

- ◆ **Possible questions for the Feminine:**
    - ◊ What does she like?
    - ◊ What does she dislike?
    - ◊ What does she love?
    - ◊ What does she hate?
    - ◊ What depletes her?
    - ◊ What gives her energy?
    - ◊ What really pisses her off?
    - ◊ For what does she feel responsible?
    - ◊ What overwhelms her?
    - ◊ Of what does the Feminine need more?
    - ◊ Of what does she need less?
    - ◊ How does she feel about the Masculine?
    - ◊ What does she feel about the Child?
    - ◊ What makes her feel disrespected and undervalued?
    - ◊ What allows her Feminine energy to feel recognized and respected?
    - ◊ What keeps her in her integrity and truth?
    - ◊ What makes the Feminine feel adored and appreciated?
    - ◊ What makes her feel acknowledged and accepted?

◆ **Possible questions for the Masculine:**
- ◊ What does he like?
- ◊ What does he dislike?
- ◊ What does he love?
- ◊ What does he hate?
- ◊ What makes him feel disrespected and unappreciated?
- ◊ For what does the Masculine feel responsible?
- ◊ What angers him?
- ◊ What over burdens him?
- ◊ What frustrates him?
- ◊ What does he think about the Feminine?
- ◊ What does he think about the Child?
- ◊ Of what does the Masculine need more?
- ◊ Of what does he need less?
- ◊ What makes him feel secure and in control?
- ◊ What makes him feel appreciated?
- ◊ What keeps him in his integrity and honor?
- ◊ What pleases the Masculine energy?
- ◊ What makes him feel honored and respected?

◆ **Possible questions for the Child:**
- ◊ What does the Child like?
- ◊ What do they dislike?
- ◊ What do they love?
- ◊ What do they hate?
- ◊ Is the Child getting enough time to play?
- ◊ How does the Child want to play?
- ◊ Of what does the Child need more?
- ◊ Of what does the Child need less?
- ◊ How does the Child feel about the Feminine?
- ◊ How does the Child feel about the Masculine?
- ◊ Does the Child understand that they are not responsible for any life changing decisions?
- ◊ Does the Child know that their job is to be innocent and playful?
- ◊ What makes the Child feel safe?
- ◊ Is there enough fun and laughter in the Childs life?
- ◊ Do they need more affection?
- ◊ Do they need more nurturing?

- ◆ After both the Feminine and the Masculine have been heard in this Council session and neither one has anything more to say, invite in the Self.

- ◆ Possible questions for the Self:
  - ◊ What depletes and dishonors the Self?
  - ◊ What causes the Self to be ignored?
  - ◊ What concerns the Self?
  - ◊ What nourishes the Self?
  - ◊ What does the Self need to be heard?
  - ◊ How does the Self view the Feminine?
  - ◊ How does the Self view the Masculine?
  - ◊ How does the Self view the Child?
  - ◊ How does the Self guide the Feminine, the Masculine and the Child?
  - ◊ What are the goals of the Self?
  - ◊ What does the Self need to flourish?
  - ◊ What does the Self need to accomplish its purpose and mission?

- ◆ Once everyone has had a say, ask the following questions and really listen.
  - ◊ What does the **Feminine** need to flourish and prosper?
  - ◊ What does the **Masculine** need to thrive and succeed?
  - ◊ What does the **Child** need to feel safe and be happy?
  - ◊ What does the **Self** need to be a clear guiding light?

◆ **Often memories of that past may creep in as you experience the Council.**
Pay attention to these cues. Know that through the Council, you are giving yourself space for these are old, unconscious thoughts and beliefs to bubble up to the surface. This allows you to discern if the memory is overly influencing you in the present and whether you want to keep it alive or not. This is part of the journey. Remember, unveiling and releasing your past, can lead to pots of gold at the end of the rainbow.

◆ **With the past in mind, the following questions may be useful:**
  ◊ What crucial roles did your mother, father, siblings, grandparents, family members, teachers, mentors and other significant people play in the development of your Feminine?

  ◊ What crucial roles did your mother, father, siblings, grandparents, family members, teachers, mentors and other significant people play in the development of your Masculine?

  ◊ What crucial roles did your mother, father, siblings, grandparents, family members, teachers, mentors and other significant people play in the development of your Child?

  ◊ What crucial roles did your mother, father, siblings, grandparents, family members, teachers, mentors and other significant people play in the development of your Self?

  ◊ What crucial roles did these people play in the distortion of each of these energies? In other words, what hindered the development of your Feminine, your Masculine, your Child or the Self?

  ◊ What wounds did you suffer from their hands?

  ◊ How did these distortions affect each of these aspects?

  ◊ How did they hinder or restrict your healthy development of becoming a powerful and authentic woman?

- ◊ How did your mother, father, siblings, grandparents, family members, teachers, mentors and other significant people in your life influence the development of your Self worth?

- ◊ How did your upbringing influence the positive development of your integrity, confidence and sovereignty?

◆ **Are there any other events, experiences or childhood memories that affect the Feminine, the Masculine, the Child or the Self?**
Include significant relationships, siblings, family members, marriages, divorces, deaths, births, ceremonies, rites of passage, legal proceedings, needs or promises kept or denied, graduations, accomplishments, failures, times of crisis, financial challenges or wins, personal struggles, betrayals, heart breaks or successes.

To End The Council:

◆ **When you feel your council is complete, spend a moment thanking all aspects of yourself for their honesty and their commitment to this work.**

◆ **If it feels appropriate, spend some time writing or journaling any nuggets of truth or realizations that may have been revealed.**
This will help to clarify the journey and empower your intent.

◆ **Take a moment to honor and acknowledge all that you just accomplished.**

By practicing your own internal Council, you will become an expert at truly listening and honoring another's opinion in your external world. At the germ of creation, the Feminine and the Masculine are balanced in each one of us, regardless of our gender. In life, as we move towards our birthright and true calling, a balance of both the Feminine and the Masculine yields fulfillment, happiness, prosperity and true abundance.

THE MOTHER OF US ALL

*Embodying the many faces, guises,
bodies and mysteries of the feminine within.*

How do I call you by name when I know not who you are?

How do I invoke your very essence when I know not where to cast the spell?

You, who are veiled in many an incarnation.

Called names, labeled, banished and revered.

Envied, worshipped yet disempowered still.

As the changing of the moon, you wax and wane, full bellied with barren lands.

The masks of our delusions clearly tattooed on your body and reputation.

Imprinted and seared, so deeply we trip on their wounds.

As I journey into you.

As I stretch my judgment so wide it cracks and splinters to its death.

Behind all the stories, the myths and lies, I ask

"Are you there in the deepest mystery?

Do you hold true?

Or are you the one who is simply playing a role in a symphony of heaven and hell?"

Gaia, Kali, Earth Mother, Bitch.

Divine Mother, Sacred Prostitute, Mother Mary.

Who stands high in the walls of our churches,

Beyond human, idealized, dehumanized.

Then what does that make us mere mortals?

If we call on you, will you answer?

Yet maybe the path is not towards you, but inward instead.

To travel far and wide in our own spaciousness of precious feminine.

To unravel and explore the demons, the angels and all the

labyrinths and ley lines in between.

You who are everything.

You who are nothing.

You who do not even care.

You are the ripe breast and the infertile womb.

You are the potent seed of life and the terrible destroyer of death.

Which means if I am born of you, if I am an aspect of you,

I too can revel in all my own glory, my sleeping passions, my rage.

What if I already behold you?

What if there is no more searching, no more seeking.

Just a simple loving embrace of welcoming you home.

The harder I grab hold of your essence, you pour like liquid gold through my hands.

As we fall back into grace, laughter roars in your belly

and you scream a searing cry to the creation and destruction of it all.

I feel you awake in me, as you breathe life and death into the strokes of my life

and I wonder...

"Is it you, my deepest mystery, who I know without knowing?
Is it you playing such a glorious, glorious game?"

I pray to give up the search.
I pray to remember I no longer need to seek you out
because you are already fully awake within me.

I pray to be still enough for you to find me.
I pray to be silent enough for you to rest in my being.

I pray for my hands, my heart, and my fear to crack open
to the grace and beauty of all of who you are.

I pray I have the courage to release all the confines of understanding you.
I pray to have the need to label you no longer.

I pray I allow myself to fall into your infinite presence in all that I am in all that I do.

I pray to release the torture of the Holy Grail, as I know your essence,
your love, your creation and destruction already is and is always within me.
I pray I remain close to the hearth of my true nature
so you will always find me home.

I will lay myself to rest.

I will allow myself to die a little, to be reborn.

I will devote my love for you over my fear.

I will embody you in a fierce and passionate love affair

and fall into the deep expanse of who I truly am.

And in the chaos of not knowing,

I will return to wonder

and succumb to your grace, wisdom and infinite power.

HOW TO DIGNIFY THE FEMININE

We are human beings, not human doings.

The aspect of *being* Feminine lies at the heart of who you are as women. When the Feminine is fully embodied and revered, a quality of the Goddess is invoked. You become a part of creation itself and at the source of this essence lies such power and grace. As a woman when you feel into the delicious softness and love of your body, you invoke the world of the Feminine. The secret is to allow this expression of you the freedom and nourishment she desires. If she is bound in producing, doing and surviving, her ability to adorn, dream, envision and nurture will be shut down. Thus not allowing the potent flame of her power to ignite and nurture you and the world around her.

STILLNESS AND SILENCE

*Standing still in time is a magical moment
allowing a deep penetration of being present.*

Stillness and silence are two qualities, which allow you to drop into the realm of the Feminine. She is ever present and by pausing and drawing your awareness inward, she is revealed. This could mean walking into an empty church or standing in your garden drinking in the sun. It may be a bath or sitting in meditation. Find your own elixir and give yourself the pleasure of receiving this gift consciously and daily, even if only for a few moments.

NO TIMELINE

A true expression of freedom.

Imagine a world where there was no time. Infinite possibility would thrive, as there would be no limit. You would be able to breathe, enjoy and be fully present to the moment, because the pressure of the 'to do' list would dissolve without the pressing need of having to accomplish it by a certain deadline.

Yet the shadow side may be that very little would be accomplished. If you had boundless time, would you still be motivated to get anything done?

It seems it is all about balance. There are moments when living in a human body and following the rhythm of time can be highly beneficial. One fact of life is that on this earth plane the physical existence of your body will end, hence time being a most precious commodity. Yet, on a spiritual realm, you are infinite energy. Therefore, it seems to be about honoring both of these aspects.

Allow your Feminine expression to have her way by carving out lengths of time with no agenda. Ideally, it could be a full day or a vacation of not having to do anything. It could even be giving yourself a morning of pottering around your house and garden or going back to bed with a cup of tea and a facemask. It is all about knowing there is nothing to do or achieve in this window. The opportunity is to just *be* and not *do*. This is then partnered up with your time spent achieving and doing, but it is coming from a place of balance because your Feminine has been nurtured and acknowledged.

CREATIVITY

Creativity by its nature needs space to grow and cultivate.

By stifling creativity, you are stifling the Feminine. If your world has been taken over by agendas and 'to do' lists leaving no room for the expression of freedom, spontaneity or creativity, then you have deeply buried your Feminine alive. You will know you have done this because your life will feel full of drudgery, responsibility and overwhelm.

Interestingly, you often need to bring in an aspect of containment, which comes from the Masculine, to carve out room for creative expression. Unfortunately, much of life is ruled by the need to survive. This more Masculine aspect of the brain will drive you to take on responsibilities and will demand the role of accountability and productivity, thus eliminating the space for the creative Feminine.

Therefore, as long as this aspect of your brain knows you are going to survive, meaning your basic needs are taken care of, it will then feel safe enough to literally plan time for creativity. By giving bookends to the allotted time, the space in between can then be filled with the luxurious freedom of whatever your heart desires.

"Often I find that to be creative I need a clean slate. Obviously, this is not always literal unless you are a fine artist. If the space I want to create in is organized, then I find there are fewer distractions. In addition, if the environment is conducive to what I am creating always helps. When I am writing, if the pen, paper, chair and desk are all ready for me and I don't have to move half a dozen things, my desire to create is fulfilled and there are less obstacles to surmount." ~ Miranda

Ways To Make Space For Creativity:

◆ Carve out this precious time. It can be part of your own personal journey, a class or in a group of people, which invokes creativity within you.

◆ Mark it in a calendar. This will help make it a physical reality rather than a vague inclination.

◆ Let people who rely on you know the plan ahead of time, so everyone is prepared for you being unavailable while you are creating.

◆ Do not fill the space, even if it feels as though the world is encroaching in on that precious jewel of time. Ignore the voice that has should or should not written all over it. Be courageous and triumph over your survival and stress levels. Spend this valuable time expressing your creativity.

◆ Notice how you feel afterwards.

◆ Remember this feeling to remind yourself why you are going to create again.

"When my daughter was born, my world of time, responsibility and creativity all channeled to her. Often her father would come home at the end of the day and I would still be in my pajamas. He would ask, "What have you been doing?" To be honest I did not really know. Yes breast-feeding, yet I seemed to spend hours just cuddling or looking at her. She seemed such a miracle to me and for once in my life, time seemed to be standing still. Yet after about six months, I started to get a little homebound. The aspect of me that was not a mother needed some expression. I could feel her. "This is all well and good, but is this it?" she kept nagging at me, and I chose to listen. I found a pottery class and went once a week. It was three hours of a different kind of bliss and it allowed my 'Self' to remain balanced in my mothering as I was able to express the other parts of who I am." ~ Miranda

ADORNMENT AND SENSUALITY

The Feminine is the adorner of the earth.

Have you ever noticed that when you put on a certain pair of shoes or perfume that you feel more Feminine? Women are the adorners. The Feminine desires flowers on the kitchen table and a soft, cashmere throw on the sofa. It is not about practicality at this point, but about enhancement and beauty.

"When I walk into a house that is clean and also aesthetically beautiful to my senses, I find I can relax and breathe easier. It brings me such pleasure. My family always laughs at me after my fabulous housekeeper leaves. I am so happy everything is spotless, and the beauty of my home is clear to me." ~ Miranda

When you permit yourself the time to express this part of the Feminine, it allows her energy to flow. Obviously, there are times when to be wearing comfortable or practical work clothes are appropriate. Yet when the chore or work is completed, it is then time to focus on adorning the Feminine. This will change your mood, your outlook and everything about you. It is amazing what lighting an aromatherapy candle, taking a bath or even wearing certain underwear can do for the senses!

Take some time each day to embellish yourself and your environment. This can be as simple as listening to music, lighting some incense or choosing to wear some earrings you love.

Also, pay attention to the world of saving time and practicality. If you are not careful, they will dictate your whole existence and extinguish any ember of sensuality. It is all about balancing this with downtime and creativity.

A CLEAN SLATE

An artist needs a clean canvas to create a masterpiece.

For the Feminine to be able to relax and be at peace, her environment plays a role. When the surrounding space is clean, organized and aesthetically pleasing, you will find that your ability to create, rest and have fun is greatly enhanced. Needless to say, a perfectly clean space is not always available. Sometimes you have to triumph over the need for order and choose to create, play or rest anyway.

"To be honest, if I had to wait for the canvas to be blank in order to paint, it would never happen, figuratively speaking." ~ Miranda

NATURE AND SPIRITUALITY

Spirituality holds nature in her hands.

Both of these extraordinary aspects of life can invoke and support the Feminine.

Nature, by her very essence, is all about creativity and rhythm, the waxing and waning of the moon and the tides, the blossoming and growth of flowers and fruits. Yet all of these natural occurrences are also supported by the Masculine. As with all of life, it is about the polarities living in balance with each other.

Ways To Connect To Nature:

- Choose to spend time in nature, even if it is just for a few moments. Go outside in the sun or the rain. Look at the sky or clouds or a blossoming flower. Plant your feet into the earth and take a few deep breaths.

- Instead of ignoring natural rhythms, consciously choose to flow with them. As the sun sets, start to slow down your day and go inward. This will give you a good night's sleep and reward you with the energy to begin the next day with the rising sun as nature intended.

- Allow nature to lead you. Perhaps on your day off, you planned a busy morning of chores and running around. Yet when you awoke, it was pouring with rain. This could be seen as a gift of giving you permission to stay cuddled up in bed with a good book or a phone call. This will mean the 'to do' list will have to wait. Yet strangely enough, life carries on quite well even when not everything is accomplished.

- Spirituality tends to bring in a sense of inner calm and peace that can help reduce the internal or external chatter and the business of the mind. In these moments, a deeper sense of who you are is present and often the true Feminine is revealed.

Ways To Invoke Spirituality:

- Pray, meditate and invite in whatever spiritual practice resonates with you. This will help you to drop inward and connect to the infinite source of creation that you truly are.

- Be deeply grateful for all you have. Gratitude is a fertile foundation to create the life you truly desire. No matter how dire life seems, there is always something for which to be grateful.

- Find communities and rituals that allow you to express your spirituality.

HONOR ALL ASPECTS OF THE FEMININE

By acknowledging all aspects of the Self, we become whole.

This includes the Bitch, the Queen, the Crone, the Lover, the young Child, and the wayward Teenager. For example, if your Bitch is on a rampage, there is probably a good reason and it often boils down to not taking care of yourself. When prioritizing everyone else has reached its crescendo, then some part of you has to express itself and who better than the inner Bitch who plays anger and resentment so beautifully. Do not ignore her or her rebellion. She has something to say and often it is for your highest good, even if she is not delicate with her approach.

Next time honor taking care of yourself more and she will not have to come out with such a vengeance.

NOURISHING AND NURTURING

Choosing love over judgment.

Imagine a tiny baby and all of a sudden, she starts to wail. Loud, ear-piercing cries fill the room. In this moment, what is it that this little one needs? Maybe she is hungry or needs to be changed. Possibly, she is afraid that there is no one around. Yet the bottom line is that as long as someone goes to her and cares for her needs, the cries will stop.

The wailing and crying of adults is usually done silently on the inside. Therefore, it does not get responded to. Unfortunately, most adults have been successfully groomed out of expressing themselves so clearly. Through eloquence and societal etiquette, you have been taught to express yourself through your words, which can be highly effective or possibly taught to control your emotions.

Yet sometimes the longing for nurturing and nourishing which lies deep within you, can be stifled and therefore not met.

The Feminine is the mistress of nurturing. As mothers, it is instinctual, as friends it is natural, as a family member it is expected. It is a natural occurrence to respond lovingly to a situation, which needs comfort. Whether it is to hold the wounded in loving arms, to stroke their head, to soothe and comfort their fears. In these moments of nurturing another, they are filled, quieted and contented to know they are seen, loved and taken care of. Just like the baby. Yet from this perspective, it is vital that the nurturer is also nourished.

Imagine a water tower that supplies a village. Day after day, the people gratefully go to the tower and fill up their water containers to quench their thirst and nourish their beings. Yet no one is filing the water tower. There is no consciousness or system to replenish it. Eventually the water dries up. Everyone suffers.

What you will find is the more you nourish and nurture yourself, the more bounty you will have to give and it will be given without resentment. This is being of service.

Ways To Nourish And Nurture Yourself:

- Honor your natural sleep patterns and rest when you are tired.

- Eat nourishing and nurturing foods as often as needed and drink plenty of water.

- Move your body daily in a way that releases stress and keeps the structure strong and vital.

- In translation, honor 'The Foundational Trinity.'

- Nourish and nurture your body. Find your own medicine that allows you to feel pampered and luxuriate in taking care of this precious temple.

- Spend some time each day connecting to you. This could be some quiet time hiking in nature or meditation. Just for a moment stop the flow of life, sit in stillness and be present to the now.

- Spend quality time with people who give to you and share a natural flow of give and take.

- ◆ Listen to music, dance or watch a brilliant movie. Find what external experience fills you to overflowing.

- ◆ Adorn yourself and your living environment daily. This can be as simple as a beautiful scarf or a cut rose.

- ◆ Discover what nurtures you and consciously bring it into your living experience and daily routine.

RECEIVING LIFE FORCE

Allow yourself to receive blessings.

The Feminine can be beautifully enticed by receiving life force. Prana or Chi, as it is also known, is all around you. Nature is especially potent. Have you ever noticed when you are standing on a cliff, with huge waves crashing and a spray on your face, how you feel? The chances are you became more revitalized and alive. You, in that moment are receiving the life force from the sea. It is similar to when you stand in the sun for a few minutes and bask in the warmth, light and energy this gives. Just as a flower receives life force from the sun, so do humans.

Another conscious way to receive this energy is through certain movements. Yoga and martial arts, such as Tai Chi, are direct pathways to this life force. For some it may be hiking in nature or being in water. Yet the point is, as you move, the body rebalances, releases tension and stress and you are literally making space for new energy to enter. Think of a hosepipe with a kink in it. Nothing flows through. Yet when you undo the blockage, the flow is re-established.

Spend a moment contemplating what fills you. It will probably be enjoyable and you will be aware of how good you feel afterwards.

"During one of the yoga classes I teach, there is sometimes humorous resistance to how hard the sequences are. Yet I hear repeatedly how different, relaxed, energized and centered they all feel afterwards. The beauty is that by remembering this outcome, they are motivated to come back each week, even if they may not feel like it at the end of a long day." ~ Miranda

HONORING YOUR FEMININE

Receive the nurturing mystery
of the feminine as a beloved friend.

Now that you have some choices around invoking the Feminine aspect of your being, give yourself some time to contemplate your own personal relationship with this precious essence. You may be surprised by the honesty of your responses.

Ask Yourself The Following Questions:

◆ Do you feel you are in relationship with your Feminine?

◆ Do you find that you tend to ignore her?

◆ How do you feel about her?

◆ What is your reaction to the realization that it is important to nourish her?

◆ How do you unconsciously connect to her?

◆ How could you consciously connect?

◆ What feeds her and ultimately you?

HOW TO EXALT THE MASCULINE

Let him protect you, provide for you and be the strong solid presence that in your hour of need you can lean on.

Each and every one of you embodies both the Feminine and Masculine. Immaterial to what gender you were born, everyone has an aspect of the Masculine. If you ignore or dishonor this part, you will be living your life out of balance.

When it comes to the stability and integration of the Feminine and Masculine aspects of the self, it seems as though there are three possibilities.

First, either the Feminine or Masculine is ignored or the other is overly developed. Again, this has nothing to do with gender. There are plenty of very Feminine men in the world.

Secondly, a distorted or corrupted view of either the Feminine or Masculine is played out. This is often comes from a childhood wound and the insult or story is still being cherished as a reality. Unfortunately, what happened in the past is often not the best reaction point to leap from in a present situation!

Thirdly, there is a conscious balance between these two extraordinarily and powerful aspects of the Self and this awareness allows for productive and aligned choices in life. There are times when the energy and drive of the Masculine are right action and other moments where the creativity and nurturing of the Feminine is perfect. When the wrong persona is in play, it is similar to trying to brush your teeth or write with the wrong hand. You are literally handicapping yourself.

From the perspective of 'A Woman's Truth', it is about aligning with the latter to live a full, prosperous, and creative life with both of these aspects in partnership, lovingly and consciously supporting each other. Imagine that!

HONOR 'THE FOUNDATIONAL TRINITY'
This will truly support the Masculine.

Getting enough rest, food and exercise is vital. Then the Masculine has the energy needed to accomplish what is at hand. To be acutely aware of your needs and choosing to meet and honor them is a strength of the Masculine. It is natural for the Masculine energy to prioritize basic human survival needs.

"For years I was called camel by my family, as I would go for hours without peeing. Sometimes, I would be so immersed in what I was doing, that to break to go to the bathroom seemed unimportant. Yet what I noticed, as I got older is I would think in my head, 'I will just finish this or wash or move that...then I will pee.' At this point my bladder would be screaming at me and it is blatantly obvious that I am not listening nor taking care of myself or my needs." ~ Miranda

ALLOW THE MASCULINE TO SUPPORT THE FEMININE AND VICE VERSA
Balancing the Yin and the Yang.

As long as both aspects of the Feminine and Masculine are being nourished and honored, then for one to support the other is a perfect partnership, just as in a healthy and loving relationship. The trouble begins when the body as a whole is not being taken care of and you have been to bulldozing through life, pulling too strongly on the Masculine drive to get you through. This tends to exhaust the Masculine and leaves no expression for the Feminine.

"Often when I am writing from my creative Feminine, I find that it is my Masculine that aligns with her to support the space by making me extremely focused. It is as though the juice is pouring out of my Feminine, yet my Masculine is directing it to where it needs to go. In this case, pen to paper and if someone disturbs me, it is as though I have to pull myself away. I now know how men feel when talked to during a playoff!" ~ Miranda

SELF-RELIANCE

No man is an island, yet knowing you could survive on a deserted one certainly helps when you are having a challenging day.

In life if you feel you can only survive by being dependent on others, you will tend to give up your power to these pseudo-saviors. Obviously everyone has to rely on someone once in a while, yet by knowing you have the ability to support and take care of yourself by its very nature, is extremely empowering. It is vital to know that if push comes to shove, you are capable and able to support, protect and nurture yourself. This strength and resolve will come from the Masculine.

"My daughter recently announced to me that she wanted to have babies and make pies. My response was that this was a genius plan, but first she would need to go to college, get a job and understand, to the core of her being, of what she is capable Once she knew this about herself, then pies and babies would be a wonderful life."
~ Miranda

GRATITUDE

Gratitude is the potent fertilizer for all dreams to manifest.

When you are deeply appreciated, an overwhelming desire to help more is ignited. Compare this to going out of your way for someone and you do not even get a thank you. Chances are you will decide not to do that again. All of your aspects thrive on appreciation, yet for the Masculine, it seems that gratitude feeds him on such a level, that it ignites generosity and going the extra mile, in a way that can be quite awe inspiring.

*"Wear gratitude like a cloak
and it will feed every corner of your life."*
~ Rumi

CONFIDENCE

By having confidence, regardless of the situation you will clearly see the path ahead and walk courageously forward.

The Masculine by its nature needs to have confidence to show up in the world and be present to conquer and win. Self-loathing and not taking care of yourself will always undermine your ability to shine in your own strength and power, ultimately diminishing your ability to assert yourself. This is not about being uncaring or unthoughtful to others. It is about walking through your life with your head held high, your shoulders back and self-assurance to your step. This lets everyone know who you are, even yourself, and that you are not afraid to live or speak your truth.

"I have to say as I grow older, with many years of life experience behind me, there is a newfound confidence to my being. The gift is I no longer care what others think as long as I am living in my own authentic integrity and wisdom." ~ Miranda

NURTURING

Even the Masculine needs to be held sometimes.

Just as the Feminine is the mistress of nurturing, the Masculine in his own way nurtures and protects constantly. What is important here is that the Masculine himself gets to receive enough nurturing. Imagine a warrior continuously in battle, he returns home weary, wounded and exhausted by the harsh realities of war. As he spends his time healing his wounds and replenishing his exhausted being, the Feminine tends to him, loves him, nurtures him and fills him again. I hope that your life is not as dramatic as this image; yet know that after a hard day's work, the Masculine needs to be taken care of, given some down time and some space that is not about achieving, but more about receiving.

BE CLEAR, CONCISE AND TO THE POINT
Stay focused!

The Masculine wants to know what the result is. Therefore, when you ignite this part of you, it will be for very specific and goal-oriented situations. When you need to get a job done by a certain deadline, call in the Masculine.

"In my relationships with men there are certain behaviors I have that tend to drive them crazy. One of the main culprits is I will mention I am tired and need to go to bed. In my head this means I will potter around for a little while, tidying up on the way, get some water and meander up to wash my face, teeth, floss and anything else I deem highly important. It is obvious I am tired and for me to be a decent human being the next day, I need to get enough sleep. Through the eyes of the Masculine, straightening the cushions is not as important as getting enough rest. Therefore, it seems as though I am sabotaging the destined result. The other area that seems to cause problems is trying to leave the house. There are always a few things I need to do along the way. The men in my life are ready, standing there with keys in hand, very Masculine. I, on the other hand, am being dictated to by the journey to the back door, whether it is putting the phone back on the hook or turning the dryer on. Sound familiar? Yet, recently I had to leave the house early. I awoke, ignited my Masculine, steam rolled my way through getting ready and was even fifteen minutes early. I am sure the men in my life wish I would invoke this aspect more often!"

NO DISTRACTIONS
Blinders are sometimes a good idea to be to avoid the shiny things in life!

When you are in the more Masculine mode of focusing and accomplishing, it is important that you are not pulling yourself in too many directions.

"When I am in my more Masculine work mode, I find that if someone interrupts me I get frustrated very easily. It is as though they are pulling me off my center and it will take work and effort to get back there." ~ Miranda

SAYING NO

With some practice, this ultimately will become your best friend.

The energy of the Masculine tends to be less emotional than the Feminine. Because of this lack of emotional response to a situation, it is much easier for the Masculine to think about a circumstance or a request in a practical and linear way. This allows the response to be a yes or a no, based on whether the situation is actually right action and a win-win situation. Hence saying no would be a perfectly acceptable response.

By invoking this more Masculine aspect of the Self, your ability to say no will be strengthened and any feelings of guilt or should's will no longer be fed by the Feminine. As you may have noticed, the Feminine is an expert at pushing her way into situations fueled by guilt and then silently resenting it afterwards. The Masculine on the other hand would just say no in the beginning without any emotional charge.

HUMILITY

Do not to confuse humility with weakness.

This is an extraordinary quality when fully lived and expressed. It is the ability to be humble, while still holding your power. It is the strength to speak your truth, live in your honor, yet still be aware of the impact your presence has on those around you. It defies shame, guilt and belittling. By its nature humility stands strong, yet love and gratitude are its source of nourishment.

The most handsome and best-attired man is the one clothed in humility.

HONORING YOUR MASCULINE

*Allow the power and might of the masculine
to provide the support and structure you dearly need.*

As you form a stronger relationship with the Masculine, give yourself some time to contemplate your personal relationship with this sometimes-misunderstood aspect.

Ask Yourself The Following Questions:

◆ Do you feel you are in relationship with your Masculine?

◆ Do you find that you tend to ignore him?

◆ How do you think or feel about him?

◆ What is your reaction to realizing that it is important to honor him?

◆ How do you unconsciously connect to him?

◆ How could you consciously connect?

◆ What feeds him?

HOW TO CELEBRATE THE CHILD

Imagine holding this aspect of yourself in your loving arms and an open heart, just as you would a young baby.

This aspect of the Self can be complicated. If the Child is ignored, your spirit of play and spontaneity will diminish to an ember, life will become dull, mundane, and work orientated. Yet if she is given too much power, your will and discipline to take care of yourself will be overrun by the desire to play and eat cake! Therefore, as with the aspect of the Feminine and Masculine, it is all about retaining balance.

The good news is that if your Feminine and Masculine are in partnership with each other, they will intuitively know how to take care of the Child and there will be a natural ebb and flow between the responsible adult and the playful carefree innocence of the Child.

"As I look back at my teenage years, it is with a deep sense of gratitude that I am still alive. In hindsight, it was a lethal combination of attitude, rebellion, the ability to drive, to buy alcohol and the belief that I knew it all. The transition from Child to adult is fraught with danger. Because the wisdom of the adult is not yet developed, there is not enough life experience, yet unfortunately my immature teenager was still in control of many of my choices!" ~ Miranda

Research has shown that the human brain does not stop developing until twenty-five. Maybe this gives a clue as to some of the strange decisions made in the early part of adulthood!

From the perspective of the adult, it is therefore imperative that when the Child aspect of the self is to be expressed, the situation needs to be appropriate. Obviously, this would not be during an important work meeting or a silent meditation. It is more about carving out certain times that you can let go of the 'to do' list and allow yourself to go and explore, play or have an adventure.

"It is curious to me that in an emotionally stressed or charged situation, such as funerals, that it is the baby or Child who often cries and acts out. My conclusion is that someone needs to release the tension and the little one has not yet been trained to stuff her emotions down and be quiet. In fact, it is quite the opposite. To wail and cry is a baby's way of communicating and if she feels discomfort she will let you know." ~ Miranda

The beauty of invoking the Child aspect is that she will keep you young, help you by not taking life too seriously and will encourage you to laugh and play. She can also be a powerful source for your creativity, whether it is through writing, drawing dancing or singing. She can also surprise and inspire you. Remember that you always have your adult aspect present to guide and facilitate if needed. The beauty of being an adult in touch with your Child is that you can safely explore the world of childhood fantasy with the parents always present to take care of you.

PLAY

Hey diddle diddle, the cat and the fiddle, the cow jumped over the moon.
The dog laughed to see such fun, and the dish ran away with the spoon.

All too often adults forget to play. The responsibility and duty of life takes over and the spontaneous, carefree aspect is squelched. Explore how you love to play. It may be in water or a game. Seek out others who want to play and carve out time specifically for carefree adventures. Let the adult be responsible, so the Child can play freely.

One of the most detrimental situations that can occur is when the Child aspect thinks it needs to do the parenting or be the adult. Just as a nine year old is unable to reach the pedals in a car or to see over the steering wheel to drive, it is also too young and underdeveloped to make big decisions about grown up life. It is not the responsibility of the Child to figure out how to pay the bills or get enough sleep. That is the job of the mature and wise Feminine and Masculine.

The impact of a dysfunctional upbringing can leave an imprint on the Child. This leaves them with an overly developed sense of responsibility. Unfortunately, from this perspective, the Child is often limited and fear based, because the psyche did not have the tools or life experience to make decisions that were right action. It will be clear when this dynamic is playing out because the choice may very well be reactionary, rather than calmly choosing to act.

"In my Childhood I was left with the responsibility of caring for a sick parent at a very early age. Even though I did the best job I could with the tools I had, it left a strong impression on my psyche. Whenever I am faced with a decision that feels overwhelming, which I am sure taking care of a sick father at age nine was, I seem to lose my mature wisdom and a sense of fear takes over. I now know that this is my triggered Child, who still has the imprint that she has overwhelming responsibilities. After much soul searching and inquiry, I have learned how to talk her off the ledge. I remind myself that I am a perfectly capable adult, who does know how to handle the situation and has the ability and insight to know what to do. It sometimes takes a moment to unwind myself, but by being aware of this dynamic, I can then find a different and wiser solution." ~ Miranda

Where in your life are you allowing or expecting the Child aspect to take over for you, when in reality the grown up would do a much healthier job? It will usually feel very out of control, yet with awareness, a new way of being can be instilled.

The other area to be aware of for those of you who are parents, is when your Child aspect is ignored for too long and becomes angry or resentful. At this point, she may decide to go into battle with your physical offspring. This is not a pretty or sought after outcome. Again, with insight and clarity you can become aware of this dynamic and choose to disengage. It is a sure sign that your internal Child needs some attention and it is good to know that walking away in that moment is the best way to go.

"It was disturbing for me to realize that sometimes my internal Child was actually jealous and resentful of the Childhood I am giving my daughter. Although on some level, it does make sense because in reality, what my daughter is experiencing is a very different life. The mother part of me who loves my daughter beyond reason, could not comprehend that I could experience such emotions toward her.

Who wants to be jealous and resentful of their own Child? Yet, with the knowledge that I do feel this way from time to time and choosing to let go of the judgment surrounding it, I can then accept this reaction. I can be acutely aware of my angry Child or teenager who wants to go into battle with my daughter.

At this point, I stop and choose not to interact, saying we will talk later when I am calmer. I then go and do something for myself, that connects me back to my center and nurtures my Child. This then reminds me that my internal Child is not responsible for my daughter. That in fact it is dangerous and inappropriate to allow her to become powerful enough to be involved in parenting. Yet I now know that when this conflict occurs the chances are I have been mothering and working excessively. By bringing some laughter and play back into my life I can carry on without too much damage control or hurt feelings." ~ Miranda

INNOCENCE AND WONDER

when innocence is lost, turn to wonder.

These two aspects of the Child are paramount to being happy. When innocence is lost, cynicism often steps in. Obviously too much innocence or not enough street smarts can get you into all sorts of trouble, yet as long as the wise adult aspect is present, this allowing of innocence is vital.

If you imagine the opposite of innocence as corruption, this gives a taste of why it is imperative to keep the pure part of your being alive, just as you would a young Child, protected from the harshness and brutality of the world. There is suffering in life and realities that can make your skin crawl. Yet, there is also extraordinary beauty and goodness present in the world. By invoking the feeling of innocence, you will allow yourself to look at the world in awe and wonder again, as you did as a young child.

As you may have noticed, the word awful stems from the word awe. One of its meanings is to be full of amazement and admiration; therefore, this is not necessarily a negative perception, as it is so often depicted today.

what in your life recently filled you with wonder and awe?

If you have no recollection or memory, maybe it is time to bring these qualities back into your life. A beautiful sunset, swimming dolphins or whales, a full moon, an exquisite flower, a new born child, a church bell, the sound of a choir singing, a waterfall or a person praying.

Would these fill you with awe and wonder?

◆ What fills your heart?

◆ What makes you stop long enough to pause, be still and stare, for the sheer beauty of it?

◆ What is your wonderland?

LAUGH

If we cannot laugh at ourselves, all is lost.

You may have noticed the more stressed you become, the less funny life is. When you are tired, overwhelmed and stressed it is hard to see the lighter side. Therefore, having people who make you laugh in your life is imperative. Also choosing a funny book or movie, instead of some dire tragedy can help. Find a way to lighten your load and elevate your mood. Yet most importantly, laugh at yourself. By being able to find humor in your situation, your perspective will change and often a more loving solution may reveal itself…seriously!

BE PRESENT

The essence and potency of now.

Have you ever noticed how children get lost in the moment of their imagination or activity? Time has no relevance, nor does the world around them. They are not worried about consequences as they are truly in the moment; present, immersed and fully alive.

◆ When was the last time you allowed for this feeling?

◆ When did you last let your hair down, kick off your shoes and run wildly just for the fun of it?

TAKE TIME

A wrinkle in time.

A time line will demolish any childlike inclination. Its presence suffocates and squeezes out laughter, play and spontaneity. Therefore, if you are in need of expressing your Child, carve out a good chunk of time so the experience is not limited or squelched just as the playing gets good.

KEEP LEARNING

Curiosity may have killed the cat, but it keeps the human brain alive.

It has been shown that keeping the brain active will help with memory and your ability to stay sharp and focused. All you need to do is just spend some time watching a small child with its insatiable curiosity as its brain develops. When you stop being curious about life, much of the world's potential and possibilities die. It is in the curiosity that the new is discovered and challenges and adventures come alive.

Remember that change is the only constant a human being has, even though it is the one thing feared the most. Curiosity and learning give you the tools needed to ride the wave of change with an air of adventure rather than dread.

"Sometimes when I am with a client, they will talk about their desire to learn a new language. In this moment, they come alive. It is as though the world opened up for them, as an old dream could possibly become a reality." ~ Miranda

Take a moment to ponder whether there is a deep desire in you to learn or experience something new. What would this adventure be? What you are inquiring into here is an activity that would excite and fulfill you. If it even has the aftertaste of a chore, it will not last or feed you the same way.

REST

The fountain of youth.

Have you noticed how children and puppies will run around in a mad frenzy of energy and in the next moment collapse into a deep relaxed and exhausted sleep?

For the Child aspect of the Self to emerge and have the energy and impulse to play you need to be rested. For the fountain of youth to flow, the body, mind and spirit need to be replenished and filled. One of the most productive ways is to get enough rest. This could be about getting the full quota of sleep you need, but also giving yourself the luxury and permission to nap can be just as effective.

"When my daughter was little, we would go to birthday parties and of course she would eat copious amounts of sugar. When we got home, she would still be wired like a spinning top. At the time, we lived in a house with a beautiful large kitchen with a butcher's block in the center. I would encourage her to run around the butcher's block to release all the sugar energy. She would do this quite hysterically twenty to thirty times until exhaustion would make her drop. At this point, I would scoop her up, brush her teeth and gratefully tuck her into bed, knowing she would then sleep off the sugar hangover." ~ Miranda

HONORING YOUR CHILD

*Invite the innocence of your heart-felt child
to lighten your life and welcome the joy of wonder and play.*

Now that you have some choices around embracing the child aspect of your being, give yourself some time to contemplate your own personal relationship with this often confusing side of yourself.

Ask Yourself The Following Questions:

◆ Do you feel you are in relationship with your child?

◆ Do you find that you tend to ignore your playful side?

◆ How do you feel about play?

◆ What is your reaction to realizing that it is important to nourish your imagination and creative aspect of yourself?

◆ How do you unconsciously connect to your child?

◆ How could you consciously connect?

◆ What feeds your child?

HOW TO REVERE THE HIGHER SELF

Be still and listen.

In order to hear the quiet, yet profound guidance and voice of the Higher Self you need to be still long enough to actually listen. Often, the wailings of a wounded child or the voice of an angry, overly tired woman will be louder in your head and will override the calm, internal voice of wisdom. The feeling of knowing right action is always available, it is just whether you choose to acknowledge or ignore its wisdom.

An old Cherokee told his grandson, "There is a battle between two wolves inside us all. One is evil. It is anger, jealousy, greed, resentment, inferiority, lies and ego. The other is good. It is joy, peace, love, hope, humility, kindness, empathy and truth." The boy thought about it for a while and asked, "Which wolf wins"? The old man quietly replied, "The one you feed". The following are guidelines that will allow you to be in your center long enough to listen, to hear and to follow the intuitive guidance of the Self.

BE STILL ENOUGH TO LISTEN

The sound of silence.

If you are overwhelmed and running two thousand miles an hour, the chances of *hearing*, let alone listening are minimal. Yet, to pause long enough to know there is a choice in the paths ahead will delay the rollercoaster and allow you to make the most beneficial choice. If you do not stop to listen, how can you know silence?

"What is truth? A difficult question; but I have solved it for myself by saying that it is what the 'voice within' tells you."
~ Gandhi

STAY IN YOUR INTEGRITY AND BE YOUR TRUE SELF

Learn to say no.

When you pause long enough to hear, you can then align yourself with this guidance even if this means saying no or displeasing someone. Remember if you are tired and resentful and you agree to a request, you are ultimately lying by saying a dishonest yes. From this perspective, you are unable to be of service to yourself or another.

SPEAK YOUR TRUTH AND BE HONEST UPFRONT

If everybody likes you, you are doing something desperately wrong.

It might seem strange to encourage you not to care if people like you, but there is freedom in this. Someone may not like you simply because of your looks, ethnicity, or sex. When you are no longer conforming to what others want you to be, there is the possibility of hurting another person's feelings. Typically, if they are used to you aligning with whatever they need, these people will find your newfound strength of truth disconcerting. Remember, being honest can be done lovingly and the brilliance is that it is the ultimate act of love to you.

"I loved turning forty. I no longer seemed to care what other people thought of me, as my own knowledge of myself felt stronger. Freedom at last!" ~ Miranda

HONOR 'THE FOUNDATIONAL TRINITY'

Sleep, movement and nutrition.

By following 'The Foundational Trinity', you will have a balance and solid foundation to find your own truth and integrity. Obviously if you are tired and hungry, the chances are you will be in reaction, far far away from your authentic True Self. To be aligned with the True Self, all your survival needs have to be taken care of, otherwise they will dominate you until they are met.

In order to be spiritual in the west, you need to be prosperous.

MEDITATION

A doorway inward.

This is about finding a way for you to still and quiet the reaches of the mind, therefore allowing the observer and witness that is always present in you, to give you a bird's eye view on whatever is going on in your life. This will enable you to know clearly which direction to take.

A hawk is circling the skies when it sees its prey eating some seeds on the ground. Yet, in its wisdom, it circles again and notices a bobcat waiting to pounce on the prey. The hawk circles to a new territory because it knows better than to become the cat's dinner.

"I am not this hair, I am not this skin,
I am the soul that lives within"
~ Rumi

HONOR YOUR HIGHER SELF

*Magnify your intuitive essence
with the grace and wisdom of divine knowledge.*

Now that you are embracing this higher aspect of the Self, give yourself some precious time to contemplate your personal relationship with this always available intuitive guide.

Ask Yourself The Following Questions:

◆ Do you feel you are in relationship with your higher Self?

◆ Do you find that you tend to ignore your intuition?

◆ How do you feel about listening to the Self?

◆ What is your reaction to realizing that it is important to nourish your intuition and to honor and listen to this inner wisdom?

◆ How do you unconsciously connect to your Self?

◆ How could you consciously connect?

◆ What feeds your higher Self?

FULL EXPRESSION OF YOUR FEMININE

Inviting in the senses to cultivate and explore the feminine.

Imagine your five senses as touchstones to your world of feminine uniqueness. By exploring any one of these qualities, a doorway into many aspects of your femininity can be revealed. A brush with silk or a cuddle with cashmere, the scent of a rose or the luxury of an aromatherapy bath, are just some examples of the luscious ways in which these perceptions invoke the feminine. In using each of the senses, which include touch, smell, sight, taste and hearing, you can take a moment to explore what images or experiences come to mind.

Just as certain sensual sounds, smells, touch or tastes are magical at appealing to the feminine, know and be aware that others are powerful at dissolving her essence. Imagine you are in a serene garden with water flowing, the smell of roses in the air, lying cushioned on a blanket of pillows with the sweet taste of honey on your lips and all of a sudden a huge loud airplane sears through the sky deafening all in its path. In that moment, all tranquility and the explosion of sound dashes serenity and grace with your more masculine aspect. It will awaken in a flash to discern if the situation proves a need to protect.

How To Use The Senses To Invoke The Feminine:

◆ **Take a moment to place yourself in the sensual world of scents and aromas.**

- ◊ Smell the perfume you are wearing on your wrist or a fragrant flower.

- ◊ Allow yourself to receive what these scents invoke in you.

- ◊ Notice how it influences your mood.

- ◊ Become aware of how this particular scent might arouse the feminine.

- ◊ What does it stir in you?

- ❖ Explore the same relationship with the sense of touch.

    - ◊ Stroke one of the fabrics you are wearing or sitting near.

    - ◊ How does its touch make you feel?

    - ◊ Find something soft or silky and lightly brush it against your skin.

    - ◊ Let the sense of touch adorn you.

    - ◊ Who do you become in that moment?

- ❖ Discover a sound, which connects you to your body and allows you to drop into the present moment.

    - ◊ It may be music, your heartbeat, a bird singing or even silence itself.

    - ◊ What does the sound arouse in you?

"Music is the mediator between the spiritual and sensual life."
~ Beethoven

- ❖ Look around and let your eyes rest on what you deem as beautiful.

    - ◊ Soften your gaze and let the sense of sight embellish your feminine heart.

    - ◊ Take your time and drink in the loveliness of what you see before you.

    - ◊ Be still and see who you become.

◆ **Find a food or a drink, which will quench your feminine thirst.**

◊ Savor the taste and texture, and like a good wine, take your sweet time.

◊ A ripe fig, a flute of champagne, fresh whipped cream, chocolate.

◊ Find your own personal, delectable journey.

◊ Relish in the intoxicating sensation of taste.

◊ Who awakens in you?

◆ **Allow all your creative, sensual and imaginative juices to flow.**
Therefore, it is in the pausing to be aware of the unconscious habits that new ways of being are born and the sensual world of your body can ignite.

Remember...

"Habit is the sixth sense that overrules the other five."
~ Arabian Proverb

REVEAL MORE TRUTH

Your real influence is measured by the treatment of yourself.

Much of the time ahead will be about partnering 'The Foundational Trinity' and 'Body Care and Symbology' as a support system to energize all the aspects of yourself. As you may have noticed, what nourishes the Feminine may not be as impactful for the Masculine or vice versa. In addition, the Child, well she is a whole other ballgame!

As you move into the world of 'Feminine Power', the journey is becoming internal. What this means is the path you are travelling is moving inward toward the Self, rather than a topic like 'Embodying Movement', which is much more practical, outwardly motivated and grounding.

- **On a daily basis, connect to a different sense and allow it to become an expression of your Feminine.**

- **Spend some time doing your own personal Council and answer the questions regarding taking care of the Feminine, Masculine, Child and Self.**
  Many answers to the questions can be revealed during this internal dialogue.

- **Consciously nurture your Feminine daily.**
  This is as simple as a dab of essential oils or buying flowers for your home.

- **Honor the needs of your Masculine daily.**
  This aspect is all about producing a result, therefore set him up so you can win, and remember, he too needs to be nurtured, fed, and given time to relax.

- **Listen to your higher Self and intuitive guidance.**
  By paying attention to this wisdom, life can become full of miracles and synchronicities.

- ◆ **Carve out time to play and create without a time line.**
  This one is probably one of the most important and fun parts of your 'Reveal More Truth'. This means no timeline, no agendas and no taking care of others. You will have to choose a space in your day and guard it with your life. This is about feeling safe enough to be free, playful, spontaneous, silly and thoroughly unproductive. The beauty of the child is that she lives in the present moment and does not need to know what will happen next. Give yourself this gift.

Remember this work together is all about falling madly and deeply in love with all parts of you. When you become judgmental, critical and overly opinionated about how you are doing, evoke the essence of the Divine Mother whose energy always holds you in love and compassion.

Wishing you my heart-felt love and plenty of play,

Miranda

ABOUT MIRANDA
A spirited guide and mentor.

Miranda is a passionate and devoted leader. Her loving and wise support will guide you on a transformational journey as her powerful teachings unveil the truth of who you are. Her gift is to offer potent tools, which inspire exquisite and beautiful self-care and empower you to live the fullest and most authentic life possible. As a mentor and guide, Miranda deeply walks her talk and is fearless about her own path of self-discovery, as she weaves the sacred into the mundane.

The simple, yet powerful premise offered by the mystic Rumi is the foundation of Miranda's philosophy and mission:

> "Never give from the depths of your well,
> always give from your overflow"

Miranda gives Council and Guidance for the Mind, Body and Spirit. With a background in Nutrition and Energy work, Miranda is the Creator of 'A Woman's Truth' and 'The Spirit of Energy', an Author, a Workshop and Retreat Leader, a Reiki Master and Yoga and Meditation teacher. Miranda studies under the guidance of her Beloved teachers Rod Stryker and Adyashanti.

To speak with or follow Miranda, please call or visit:

Phone: 626~798~6544
eMail: Info@MirandaJBarrett.com
Website: www.MirandaJBarrett.com
Facebook: Miranda J Barrett
Twitter: MirandaJBarrett

ABOUT HELENA

A visionary artist.

Helena Nelson-Reed is a visionary artist whose primary medium is watercolor. Born in Seattle, Washington, she was raised in Marin County and Napa Valley, California and today lives in Illinois. A largely self-taught artist whose educational emphasis and degree is in psychology, Nelson-Reed's primary focus is exploring the collective consciousness and the portrayal of archetypal imagery in the tradition of Carl Jung and Joseph Campbell. Rendered in luminous watercolor technique often described as ephemeral, Nelson-Reed's paintings are created in extraordinary detail, pushing the medium of watercolor past the usual limits. Her work may be found in private collections, book covers, magazines and cd covers. Nelson-Reed also has a line of jewelry, calendars and greeting cards.

Helena's Mission:

My images can be interpreted many ways, and for some will serve as portal to the mythic landscape. Descriptions providing background about each painting are available by request. Navigating and translating myth into contemporary wisdom is the traditional way of transmitting information, shamanic practice, a multi – cultural practice.

Myth, fairy, folk and spiritual lore describe divine beings and supernatural life forms arriving unbidden and disguised. In our earthly dimension, mortals often play similar roles in the lives of one another. Destinies and energies collide and interact, visible and invisible forces are at work. The mythic realms are timeless, offering insight and inspiration. While my paintings have a positive energy, many have roots in the shadows of life experience and human psyche; like the lotus blossom rooted in pond mud. For many, life is one challenge followed by the next, like beads on an endless string.

Take heart! Like goddess Inanna, one may navigate the underworld, move through dark places yet return to the realms of light battle scarred but wiser, richer for the experience. Read the ancient tales, the great mythic literature; draw strength, for they are repositories of wisdom.

Visit Helena's website for her art, for purchase information and art to wear jewelry:

eMail: HNelsonReed@Gmail.com
Websites: www.HelenaNelsonReed.com
www.etsy.com/shop/HelenaNelsonReed
Blog: www.dancingdovestudio.blogspot.com
Facebook: MorningDove Design By Helena

MIRANDA'S WORLD

*Ways to stay connected
and aligned with your truth.*

BOOKS:

A Woman's Truth
A life truly worth living.

Priceless teachings reveal your transformational
journey ahead. Obstacles to self-care are explored
as clear and loving intentions are conceived.

The Grandeur Of Sleep
Permission to rest.

Miraculous benefits are realized as the worlds of sleep,
relaxation and rejuvenation are explored and deeply honored.

Nourishing Nutrition
Reclaim your health and vitality.

Reap the bountiful rewards while eating as nature intended.
Claim your health and vitality with these simple,
yet powerful tools to nourish and heal your body.

Embodying Movement
Ground your whole being.

Restore balance in your life. Discover how to embrace
your whole being through the life-enhancing benefits of body movement.

Body Care
Cherish your body as a temple.

Learn to honor your extraordinary body
as a living temple and listen to the healing messages she whispers.

Feminine Power
Fully access your supreme birthright.

Welcome and reclaim this intrinsic privilege while living
in harmonious balance between the masculine and the feminine.

The Abundance Of Wealth
Receive the gifts of prosperity.

Understand the energy flow of prosperity and weave
the threads of abundance throughout the tapestry of your life.

Find Your Authentic Voice
The courage to express who you truly are.

Your greatest ally is born
when you courageously speak your truth and claim your unique power.

Loving Yourself
A love affair with the self.

As you become highly attuned to your own needs,
allow love to lead the way. Grant yourself permission
to honor and express your heart's truest desires.
Love yourself, no matter what.

Living A Spiritual Life
Ground your divinity here on earth.

Discover what spirituality means to you
by consciously living between the worlds of the sacred and the mundane.

Service As A Way Of Life
Ignite the fire of love to truly be of service.

By utilizing the gems of exquisite self care
on a daily basis and honoring your truth, your mission of service is born.

The Crowning Glory
Fully Rejoice in Being You.

A celebration overflowing with love,
blessings, grace and gratitude. Stand confident within
your own truth as your mind becomes of service to your heart.

The Food Of Life
The versatile vegetable.

More than just a cookbook,
a comprehensive guide for nourishing your life.

Reiki
The spirit of Energy.

An insightful guidebook full of wisdom
which introduces you to the potent and healing world of Reiki.

CARDS:

Inspiration Cards
A daily Spiritual Practice.

Sixty-Five cards with simple yet inspirational qualities
to live by and an insightful guidebook to lead the way.

CD'S:

The Grandeur of sleep and Rejuvenating Rest

An ancient healing art of rest and relaxation.

Simple yet profound practices, which alleviate stress and tension allowing your mind, body and spirit to heal, restore and replenish.

TO ORDER PLEASE VISIT:

www.MirandaJBarrett.com
www.Amazon.com

All books are available in printed or eBook form.

TESTIMONIES
to 'A Woman's Truth' teachings.

"'A Woman's Truth' is for a woman who wants to awaken her true self and embody the feminine. I have been a participant, and Miranda is a master teacher and her guidance is warm, intuitive and nurturing. She assists each woman she works with to discover the radiance that lies within themselves. I highly recommend this book series for it is a life-changing process for a woman."

Tarnie ~ Founder of 'Body Freedom' ~ Altadena, CA

"I began this book feeling as though everything feminine in me had been dulled and neglected. I was longing for a life of beauty and radiance but had little idea how to make the needed changes. In the 'A Woman's Truth' series, Miranda mapped the journey to the new life I wanted. She teaches where to begin and how to progress. The steps are gentle yet powerful, and build on each other to create a profound transformation."

Lexa ~ Lawyer and Mother ~ Pasadena, CA

"'A Women Truth' changed my life. I learned so many tools that support me in feeling healthy, taking care of myself, embodying the feminine, and most importantly, speaking my truth. Miranda is a loving, nurturing and in tuned teacher who led us step by step on how we can live the life we desire. Since reading the books, I have changed jobs for the better and am in a loving relationship. I feel more connected to myself, which allows me to go out in the world with greater strength and fearlessness. I am extremely excited about this next chapter of my life. Thank you Miranda for providing your wisdom, guidance and love!"

Janet ~ Counselor and Teacher ~ Altadena, CA

www.ingramcontent.com/pod-product-compliance
Lightning Source LLC
Chambersburg PA
CBHW080522110426
42742CB00017B/3206